Contents

THEN

Yu Li and the Heavenly Kingdom

NOW

Wang Wei and the Times of Change

Yu Li and Wang Wei

The two stories in this book are connected. One story takes place long ago and the other takes place in the present. The same object becomes important in each story for different reasons. Each main character in the stories has an adventure that occurs in the same place, but thousands of years apart.

CHINA

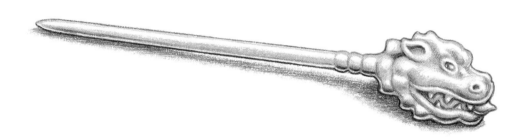

By Jean Bennett

Illustrated by Rick Powell

PICTURE CREDITS
3 (top to bottom) © Photodisc Red/Getty
Images, © Yann Layma/Getty Images; 6 Mapping
Specialists, Ltd.; 7 (top to bottom) © Brand X
Pictures/Alamy, © Dean Conger/Corbis; 45 (top
to bottom) © Giraudon/Art Resource, New York,
© Doug Houghton/Alamy; 46 (top to bottom)
© Keren Su/China Span/Alamy, © Robert
Davila/Alamy; 48 © Keren Su/Stone.

Produced through the worldwide resources of
the National Geographic Society, John M. Fahey,
Jr., President and Chief Executive Officer;
Gilbert M. Grosvenor, Chairman of the Board;
Nina D. Hoffman, Executive Vice President and
President, Books and Education Publishing
Group.

**PREPARED BY NATIONAL GEOGRAPHIC
SCHOOL PUBLISHING**
Ericka Markman, Senior Vice President and
President, Children's Books and Education
Publishing Group; Steve Mico, Senior Vice
President, Publisher, Editorial Director; Francis
Downey, Executive Editor; Richard Easby,
Editorial Manager; Bea Jackson, Director of
Design; Cynthia Olson, Art Director; Margaret
Sidlosky, Director of Illustrations; Matt
Wascavage, Manager of Publishing Services;
Lisa Pergolizzi, Sean Philpotts, Production
Managers, Ted Tucker, Production Specialist.

MANUFACTURING AND QUALITY CONTROL
Christopher A. Liedel, Chief Financial Officer;
Phillip L. Schlosser, Director; Clifton M. Brown,
Manager.

EDITORS
Barbara Seeber, Mary Anne Wengel

BOOK DEVELOPMENT
Morrison BookWorks LLC

BOOK DESIGN
Steven Curtis Design

ART DIRECTION
Dan Banks, Project Design Company

Published by the National Geographic Society
1145 17th Street, N.W.
Washington, D.C. 20036-4688

ISBN: 978-0-7922-5819-3
ISBN: 0-7922-5819-3

15 16 17 18 19 20 21 22 23
2 3 4 5 6 7 8 9 10 11 12 13

Yu Li and the Heavenly Kingdom

This story takes place in ancient China, during the rule of Emperor Wu Ti (140–87 B.C.). Yu Li's family raises silkworms. The silkworms produce silk thread. The thread is woven into silk cloth, which is sold in the market. With the money they earn, Li's family will pay their taxes to the emperor. But first they must make the long journey to the market in a northern village.

Wang Wei and the Times of Change

Wang Wei lives in modern China. Her home is in a busy city. During the school holiday she spends time with her cousin in the country. This visit helps Wei appreciate the natural beauty of China. But Wei also learns about dangers that threaten the land and wildlife.

China

China is the fourth largest country in the world. It has many different landscapes. These include mountains, plains, and deserts. China also has two famous rivers. The land along the Yangtze River and the Huang He River is fertile. It is good for growing crops such as rice and soybeans. China is also known for its giant pandas. Pandas feed on bamboo.

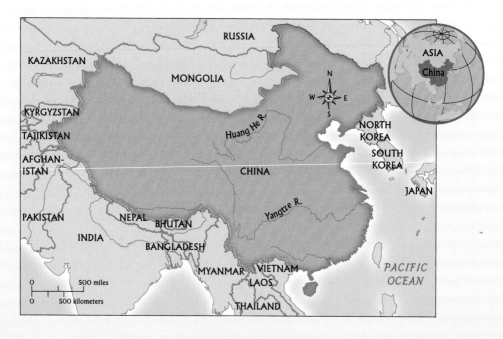

Bamboo China is the world's biggest supplier of bamboo. Bamboo is a type of grass that looks like wood. It is a good material to build with because it is light, strong, and flexible. People in China use bamboo for many things.

China: The Facts

- Size: 3,696,100 square miles
- Population: 1,306,313,812 people
- Longest River: Yangtze River
- Capital City: Beijing
- Major language: Chinese

The Yangtze River This river is the longest in Asia and third longest in the world. In 1993, China started building a dam across this river. The dam will prevent flooding and make electricity for the Chinese people.

Yu Li
and the Heavenly Kingdom

CHAPTER 1

Silkworms

Yu Li chopped mulberry leaves and heaped them into bamboo baskets. She swept back wisps of hair from her face. Then she carried the baskets to the bamboo porch. There, trays of hungry silkworms waited to munch their way through another pile of leaves.

"When will they stop eating?" she asked.

"Soon," her mother answered. "In a few days they will be ready to spin their cocoons."

Outside, her older brother, Yu Pang, and her father had taken a day off from working in the rice fields. They were making frames for the silkworm mats, where the worms would be placed to spin their cocoons.

Yu Li loved to watch the silkworms spin their cocoons, and then gradually disappear from sight surrounded by a puffy egg-shaped ball.

Yu Li had heard that many years ago, an empress had been sipping tea under a mulberry tree when a cocoon fell into her cup. The hot liquid caused the cocoon to cast off a long, delicate thread. Delighted by this, the empress gathered baskets of cocoons from the trees. She tossed them into boiling water and unravelled enough silk to weave a robe for the emperor.

Now all the rich people in China, and even far beyond the Heavenly Kingdom, wanted the fine silk that women in the villages produced. When all the thread had been woven into silken cloth, Yu Li's parents and brother would travel to a village market in the North. There her father would sell the cloth for the best price.

Each year Yu Li begged to go, but her father always said, "You are too young for the journey." This year, when she had celebrated her twelfth New Year, her father said, "In the autumn, you may go with us when we sell the silk."

Her heart leapt with excitement. She pushed aside her fear when she heard stories about wild animals and other dangers of the journey.

Within a week, the cocoons had grown puffy. One day Yu Li's mother sent her into the woods to gather firewood. By late afternoon, she had gathered a large pile of thin branches. She slung them on her back and trudged home.

In the evening, while her mother prepared dinner, Yu Li massaged her father's back. His muscles ached from guiding the water buffalo that were hitched to an iron plough. He worked all day in swampy **paddies** alongside the Yu River. She knew her father was worried about the rainy season when the swollen waters from the river spilled over the land. Sometimes, the rushing waters swept away people and animals.

When the meal was ready, Yu Li's father and Yu Pang settled on woven straw mats and ate. Yu Pang, too, had spent all day in the paddies.

After the men finished eating, they went to sit outside on the veranda. Grandmother placed

---

paddy – a wet field where rice is grown

bowls of rice and chopsticks on the low bamboo table. Yu Li, her mother, and her grandmother all sat down to eat together.

After the women finished their meal, Yu Li washed the bowls outside in a bucket of water from the village well. She could see the light from oil lamps glowing from within homes.

Yu Li left her straw sandals outside and padded over to her sleeping mat on the floor. Tired after her busy day, she quickly fell asleep.

CHAPTER 2

Weaving the Cloth

When the cocoons had been inactive for a few weeks, Yu Li's mother said, "It is time." Yu Li lit a wood fire beneath a huge iron pot of water. Soon steam rose from the water. Her mother tipped in a basket of cocoons.

Yu Li gasped. It always seemed cruel to kill such clever creatures by dropping them into hot water. Only a few were allowed to eat their way out of their cocoons and stretch their wings. Those moths would mate and the females would lay eggs. Yu Li's mother would then store the eggs in a safe, cool place until the following spring when they would hatch.

Yu Li's mother stood over the steaming pot. She loosened the silken threads and passed them through a loop on a rod above her. Yu Li reached for the fine thread. She started to wind it onto a frame. Then her grandmother collected several threads and twisted them together to make the silk strong for weaving.

Summer arrived, and the scritch-scratch sound of crickets grew loud in the warm days. Yu Li put loops of silk thread in a basket and made her way to the village dye workers.

Days later, when she returned to collect the silk, she marveled at the colors. Some of the silk had been dyed a brilliant red, a lucky color. Other silken loops were glossy shades of blue.

The finest thread had been colored a golden yellow as bright as the sun. Only royalty were allowed to wear this golden-yellow color. This silk would help to pay their taxes to the emperor.

In the following weeks, Yu Li and her grandmother did all the housework and cooking. Her mother spent every hour of daylight from sun up until sundown seated at her loom, weaving the silken threads into fine cloth.

CHAPTER 3

The Journey Begins

The rains came, and water poured down from the mountains. The water rushed over the land and into the great Chang Jiang River. The Yu River and the Chang Jiang swelled until they burst their banks, flooding the villages.

Although their village was safe on a hill, Yu Li was concerned about her father and brother working in the fields. She hoped they had escaped the floodwaters. At last, they returned home. That night, the whole family offered thanks to the river dragons for sparing their lives.

When all of the silk was woven, Yu Li's father announced, "Soon we will travel to the market village in the North."

During the next few days, Yu Li helped her mother pack salted fish, dried fruit, beans, and rice into baskets.

On the evening before their departure, the family made offerings of food to their ancestors, their family members who had died. "Oh, wise ancestors," Yu Li's father prayed, "please protect us from danger on our journey."

In the early morning light, the family balanced long poles on their shoulders. Bamboo baskets hung from each end of the poles, filled with their food and supplies for the journey and the beautiful silk cloth to sell at the market.

Their grandmother waved good-bye as they left the sleeping village. For hours they walked past paddy fields near the Yu River.

"If we were wealthy, we could sail on a boat to the market," Yu Pang said, eyeing boats on the Yu River. "It would be good to travel on the river that carries our family name."

Yu Li and her family made their way through land with reddish sandstone hills. The rich and beautiful land had earned the area the name, "Heavenly Kingdom."

Within a few days, Yu Li became used to the long hours of walking. She enjoyed the beauty of the fertile land surrounded by mountains. But when they climbed high into a forest, she felt uneasy. As they walked in the woods, she was sure she heard the rustlings of creatures.

In the evening, they stopped near a trickling stream edged by dense groups of bamboo trees. "Yu Li," her mother said, "will you please pick some bamboo shoots for us to eat with our rice?"

Yu Li nodded and pushed past the thick bamboo, searching for the fresh, green shoots. She stumbled into a clearing. A honking squeal from nearby startled her. She froze in place as a black-and-white shape rose up on hefty legs. The large animal lowered its white head and glared at her with black-rimmed eyes.

Her heart fluttered as they stared at each other. She hardly dared to breathe, waiting for the creature to lunge at her. It honked again, and she shivered. Then it slumped down and plodded away in the opposite direction.

Yu Li turned and fled as quickly as she could! Bamboo twigs scratched her arms and face, and leaves caught in her hair. She reached their camp and flung herself at her father. He listened and tried to calm her while she told him about the huge animal.

He patted her hand. "There's no need for fear," he said. "The panda is a shy creature."

Yu Li didn't sleep much that night. She lay waiting for the black-and-white panda to come and eat them all.

CHAPTER 4

The Moon Festival

The days rolled by as the family journeyed on. "Not much farther," Yu Pang said. "The market village is at the foot of the mountains." Yu Li could see the village in the distance.

"We'll be there for the Moon Festival tonight," her mother smiled. "We'll give thanks for the harvest and remember our loved ones."

As Yu Li neared the village, she noticed guards in a watchtower. They were closely watching the crowds entering the village.

"Keep your head down," her father said to Yu Pang. "The emperor's soldiers are searching for young men to serve in his army."

Yu Li's mother hurried them along until they were out of sight from the soldiers.

The narrow streets of the village were crowded with people talking in strange

languages. A man seated in a moveable chair, with two long poles in the front and back, was carried past them by his servants.

"I will find a buyer for our cloth," Yu Li's father said.

They edged past the crowds. Yu Li watched her father speak to a merchant. He showed the man their silk and the merchant named a price. Her father shook his head.

Yu Li's father then approached other merchants. After much discussion, a deal was made. The buyer moved beads on his **abacus** to calculate the total payment. Then the merchant

----

abacus – an instrument with sliding beads on rods used for counting

counted coins into her father's hand. Her father threaded the coins onto a piece of string that he tied around his neck.

"A very good price," her father said smiling with satisfaction.

After the sale of the silk cloth, they set out to explore the market. Yu Li had never seen so many beautiful objects. She saw fine paintings, bronze and gold ornaments, jewelry made from a green stone called jade, porcelain jars, and beautiful pottery.

At some stalls, herbs, plant roots, and seeds were ground into medicines and sold. Yu Li watched a man press long silver needles into the body of another man lying on a mat.

"He's having **acupuncture,**" her father explained. "The man is sick, but the healer is performing acupuncture and it will make him feel better."

Yu Li continued walking. She stopped to watch a young man bent over a scroll. With a

---

acupuncture – a Chinese practice of using needles to puncture the skin at specific points to cure disease or relieve pain brush, he drew black strokes of different shapes. He looked up at Yu Li and smiled.

"Touch it," he invited. The scroll's material was dry and rough between her fingers.

"This is called paper," he explained. "And this is writing," he said as he pointed to the symbols he had drawn.

He drew two slanting lines, leaning against each other. 人

Yu Li smiled. She looked at the young man. "It is the character for a man," he said. "This is a picture symbol."

"It looks like two branches holding each other up," she said.

"True. Just like mankind." he replied. "We need the help of others to stand tall."

Next Yu Li stopped by a stall selling finely carved jade ornaments. Her father watched her gaze at a pale green hairpin with a small, perfectly carved dragon's head. He took a coin from his string and paid the stall owner.

"It's a gift for helping your mother," he said. "The dragon will look after you."

Tears of joy pricked Yu Li's eyes. "Thank you," she said, bowing to her father.

Her mother slid the pin into Yu Li's bun. "It will keep your hair in place," she said.

They moved to an open area to watch the entertainers for the Moon Festival. The people were pleased to celebrate a good harvest. They saw jugglers toss hoops and silk balls in the air. Yu Li gasped as acrobats jumped, rolled, tumbled, and balanced on top of each other. Musicians played bells, drums, and stringed lutes.

In preparation for tonight's full moon, people were hanging lanterns. Together, Yu Li and her family prayed for the good health of her grandmother. They knew that tonight she would be looking at the moon and praying for them.

Suddenly they heard shouts. Yu Li looked up and saw soldiers pushing through the crowd. Some were dragging away young men.

"Quick! We must go," Yu Li's father said.

As they turned to escape, two soldiers caught sight of them. One grabbed hold of Yu Pang, and the other caught Yu Li by the arm.

"You'll make a fine servant girl for the empress," he sneered. "She'll pay me well when I take you to the palace."

With her free hand, Yu Li pulled her dragon pin from her hair and jabbed it into his arm. He yelled in pain.

Yu Li dragged herself free and hurried through the crowd with her parents. Just ahead, they saw the soldiers holding onto Yu Pang.

"How can we save him?" sobbed her mother.

At that moment, the ground jolted sharply beneath their feet. It rumbled as it jerked one way and then the other. *"Aeee!"* cried a man. "The sleeping earth dragon awakes."

Yu Li almost lost her balance. She clutched at her father's sleeve in terror.

"We will be all right," he reassured her. "It is only a **tremor.** The dragon is only yawning and shaking the ground as he stretches."

In front of them, Yu Li saw the soldiers let go of her brother and run away. "Yu Pang!" she called. "We're here."

He turned and ran back to them. Her father shouted, "We must go down to the river!"

They pushed through the wailing, confused crowds. On they ran until they reached the banks of the Jialing River. Waves, caused by the shifting ground, slapped at the bank. A man struggled to tie up his boat.

"We'll help you row away from here," Yu Pang called to the boatman.

----

tremor – a vibration caused by an earthquake

"And pay you well to take us home," added his father.

The family boarded the small boat. Soon they left the swirling waters behind. Once the river settled into a swiftly flowing current, Yu Li realized she was still holding her hairpin.

She touched the dragon's head. "Thank you. You protected us well," she whispered. The boat moved down the river toward their village in the Heavenly Kingdom.

Wang Wei
and the Times of Change

CHAPTER 1

Chongqing

Music boomed from outside the apartment building and woke Wang Wei. She rubbed the sleep from her eyes and looked out the window. On the nearby concrete square, dancers swayed to the music. The dancers were enjoying their morning exercise before work.

Wei wished her parents had time to join a dance group. But her mother worked long hours in a Chongqing department store. Her father worked in a shipping office by the Yangtze River and rarely came home before dusk.

Wei dressed in jeans and a red sweatshirt. She prepared a bowl of noodles and turned on the computer. She checked her e-mail while scooping up noodles with chopsticks.

Wei grabbed her cell phone and the bag she'd packed for her holiday in the country with her cousin, Gan Zheng. She locked the apartment door and walked down several flights of stairs.

Once she was outside, she saw that the usual morning fog and smog covered the mountains of the city. Dense traffic clogged the streets. Wei coughed as motorbikes drove past, leaving a trail of exhaust fumes.

A wrecking ball swung at a sagging building. It punched a large hole in the side. Dust flew into the air as the walls collapsed.

Wei turned toward the bridge across the muddy water of the Yangtze River. Cargo boats edged their way between huge tourist boats.

Wei's parents had talked about what she would do during the school holiday while they worked. Wei had rolled her eyes at the thought of weeks spent in a boring village.

But now she was on her way to the bus station. She passed a group of people doing their daily tai chi exercises. They stretched and moved like graceful animals and birds. A skateboarder zoomed past, and an old man sat on a bench beside his pet songbird in a bamboo cage.

Wei passed a group of Buddhist monks with shaved heads and brightly colored robes. They were on their way to pray at the Arhat Temple. Elderly men sat at tables outside playing cards. There was always something happening in the city. *Nothing in a sleepy little village could be as interesting as this,* thought Wei.

Wei's father had given her some yuan to spend, so Wei bought spicy dumplings from a food cart. She thought the boy cooking the food was her age. She guessed from his accent and clothes that he was from a village.

He wasn't busy, so she asked him, "Why did you come to the city?"

"There's more work here and better pay," he said. Then he added, "But I miss my family."

Wei nodded as she pulled out her cell phone. Suddenly, a small boy darted forward and snatched the phone. She chased him through the crowds.

"Stop, you thief!" she yelled, grabbing for her phone.

The boy lashed out with his foot and kicked her leg. Then he ran off. She decided that sometimes life in the city had its downside.

CHAPTER 2

The Road to the Country

At the bus station, Wei pushed her way through the crowds to get her ticket. Then she boarded the bus that would take her to the country. She looked out of the window as they passed the old city walls.

The road narrowed as they drove into the rural areas and passed paddies along the Jialing River. Wei watched a farmer lead a water buffalo through the flooded fields, pulling a plough. Farther on, she saw a boy driving goats over slippery river stones.

For hours the bus bumped over the rough roads. Wei was surprised to find herself enjoying the Sichuan Basin scenery, with its reddish sandstone hills and green fields. The fields were filled with crops of wheat, vegetables, and citrus fruit trees.

After the peaceful countryside, it was almost a shock to drive into Nanchong City amidst the honking, beeping traffic.

The sky darkened, and rain poured down as they reached the station. Wei ran for the nearest shelter, a veranda outside of an old shop.

Wei stepped onto the broken pavement, tripped, and fell forward. She struggled to regain her breath. An elderly man bent down and helped her to her feet.

"Xie-xie," she said and bowed her head to him. "Thank you."

The man guided her into his shop. She looked around and was astonished to see that the small shop was filled with lovely wooden birds and animals.

"They're beautiful," she said. She stroked the long neck of a carved bird. "This crane almost looks alive."

"If we're not more careful with our land," the old man said sadly, "this wooden bird may be the only crane we will see."

"What do you mean?" asked Wei.

"Our wildlife is dying," he explained. "The forests are being cut down, and the birds and animals are losing their homes."

Wei thought for a moment. "Do you mean we must take better care of our land?"

"*Shi,*" he nodded. "Yes."

Suddenly Wei remembered her bus. She glanced at her watch and realized the bus would leave in a few minutes.

"I must go!" she said, standing up. "Thank you again." Wei hurried back to the bus and settled into her seat.

As the bus rattled on, she caught glimpses of the Jialing River through the rain-streaked window. The rain cut channels into the hillsides, and the driver swerved to avoid rock and mud rolling down onto the road.

Wei dozed until she felt the bus slow down. The driver called to her, "This is your stop."

She picked up her bag and made her way to the exit. Outside, she stood by

the roadside in the drizzle. Then she noticed her cousin, Zheng, walking toward her.

"*Ni hao!*" she called. "Hello! I thought you'd forgotten to come."

"Sorry," he said. "It took me awhile to walk from the village."

"Do we have to walk to your home?" Wei asked in surprise. "It's wet!"

Zheng grinned. "Get used to it. And we'll need to hurry. It's getting dark."

Zheng told Wei that his grandmother would have dinner ready when they got home.

"Are your parents at home?" Wei asked.

Zheng shook his head. "They're in Langzhong City. My mother and father work in factories."

"Will they be back this evening?"

"No," he said sadly. "They're working long hours to save for my education."

Wei looked at the steep, bare hills. "Where have all the trees gone?"

Zheng frowned. "Chopped down for firewood and for buildings in the city," he said. "Now every time there are heavy rains, the landslides start."

Wei remembered what the old man in the shop had said about the forests being cut down.

Finally, they came to a scattered group of mud-brick houses. Wei saw small vegetable plots, fish ponds, and **terraced** fields.

"Over here," Zheng called to Wei.

Inside, Zheng introduced Wei to his grandmother, a little woman with bright eyes. She wore a boxy shirt and plain trousers.

Wei quickly ate a bowl of rice and vegetables spiced with hot peppers. Then they fetched water from an outside pipe and washed the dishes.

---

terrace – a flat level in a hillside made to increase farmland area and to help keep soil in place.

CHAPTER 3

Life in the Village

The following days passed in a blur. Wei fed hens and pigs, worked in the garden, and was chased by a goat with a bad temper. She jumped over a low wall to escape and was angry when she saw Zheng was watching her and laughing.

Then she began to smile, too. "I guess I've got a lot to learn about animals."

She helped Zheng's grandmother cook their meals in the evenings. She was surprised and delighted by the crisp, fresh taste of vegetables straight from the garden. Whenever she shared chores with Zheng, she found herself talking nonstop. She had often wished she had a brother or sister to keep her company. So she very much enjoyed being around her cousin.

Rain continued to fall. The ground was muddy and mist covered the hills. Wei stayed busy every day. She worked so hard that each night, her eyes closed when she lay down on her sleeping mat and didn't open until the rooster crowed at dawn.

"This is the best holiday I've ever had," she told Zheng when he showed her how to fish from the pond.

He turned to smile at her, then froze as a rumble came from the hills behind the village. Through the mist Wei saw flying rocks and thick mud tumbling down. The whole hill seemed to come crashing down in a thunderous slide, tossing boulders high in the air.

"Grandma!" Zheng yelled. He jumped up and ran toward his house.

Wei raced after him. She watched in horror as the landslide spilled over the ground like a dark river. Mud and rock showered the little garden plot where they'd last seen Zheng's grandmother working.

Zheng shouted for her. His voice was sharp with fear. They finally heard a weak answering call. They ran as fast as they could toward her voice. The old woman lay beside a low, stone wall. She was half buried. Her legs and one arm were pinned under a thick layer of mud.

Zheng and Wei quickly scooped away the dirt with their hands.

"Ouch!" Wei gasped as something dug into her finger. She picked up a hard, thin object. She slipped it in her pocket and kept on digging.

Finally Zheng's grandmother was able to sit up. She wailed in despair when she saw the damage to their crops and the few remaining hens.

"Our house is all right," Zheng said to comfort her.

They stood up and looked around the village.
One house had a large hole where a boulder had
hit the wall. Mud was piled high against several
homes. People were moving around, checking
on their stock and surveying the damage.

"I think everyone has survived," Zheng said.
He thought for a few moments. Then he added,
"This time."

CHAPTER 4

An Ancient Treasure

In the early evening, Wei and Zheng thanked their ancestors for keeping them safe. They went outside while his grandmother rested.

"The landslides will continue until we plant trees again," Zheng said. "When we do that, the roots will hold the soil firm."

"It will take years for trees to grow," Wei said.

Zheng nodded. "We have to start now."

"China is growing fast," Wei said, thinking of all the new buildings in Chongqing.

"Yes," Zheng agreed, "but we must protect nature and our farm land."

"The factories give people work, and we need the coal mines for power and fuel," Wei said. "Yet they pollute the water and air."

"There are ways to stop pollution," Zheng said. "My parents work hard so that I can go to college and learn ways to take care of the environment. It is their dream and mine."

Wei sighed. Who could ever be wise enough to sort out such big problems? She rubbed a little cut on her finger and remembered what she'd found in the mud. She felt in her pocket and examined the object under the oil lamp on the veranda. As she brushed away the dirt, she saw a finely shaped dragon's head.

"Look," she said as she showed it to Zheng.

"It's jade!" he said. "And very old."

The light-colored stone shone in the lamp light as Wei admired the delicate carving.

"How clever our ancestors were to make such beautiful things," she said.

"They were clever," agreed Zheng. "And they invented lots of things."

"Do you think our generation is smart, too?" Wei asked. "Will we find ways to make our land healthy again?"

"Yes," Zheng said firmly. "We will."

Wei looked at the darkening hills and imagined them in years to come. She saw trees covering the slopes and rivers sparkling in the fading sunlight. Wild birds and animals would return to their nesting and feeding grounds.

"Look!" said Zheng, breaking into her thoughts. He pointed to the sky.

Wei smiled as she watched a pair of cranes fly overhead. She thought of the wooden crane she had seen in Nanchong and hoped that, one day, she would see many more cranes flying in the sky.

China Then and Now

Silk Production Then

In ancient times, few people knew that silk came from the cocoons of moths. The ancient Chinese kept this secret for a long time. They tested many different

types of moths to find out which made the best silk. They found that the best silk came from a moth called Bombyx Mori.

Silk Production Now Many people now know how to make silk. It is no longer a secret art. But the Bombyx Mori is still one of the best moths for making silk. Silk is a popular fabric. It is a very comfortable fabric to wear in all temperatures.

Giant Panda Habitat Then

In ancient times, giant pandas roamed over much of the southern half of China. They lived in mountain forests and ate the bamboo that grew there. Pandas appeared in many Chinese myths and were considered a symbol of peace.

Giant Panda Habitat Now Today, the giant panda is an endangered animal. People have cut down the forests where pandas once lived. The Chinese are working to help save the remaining forests. They want to save the giant panda and its habitat.

Write a Compare-and-Contrast Essay

Think about the characters in the stories you read. How is your life similar to and different from theirs?

- Choose one of the characters, Yu Li or Wang Wei.

- Copy the Venn diagram below into your notebook.

- Use the diagram to show how your life is similar to and different from the character you chose.

- Use the example for Wang Wei below to get started.

- Write a one-page compare-and-contrast essay about how your life is similar to and different from the character's life.

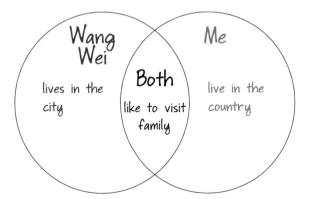

Wang Wei — lives in the city

Both — like to visit family

Me — live in the country

Read More About China

Find and read more books about China. As you read, think about these questions. They will help you understand more about this topic.

- What is the climate of China?

- Why is the Yangtze River important to the people of China?

- What were some of the customs of the people of ancient China?

- What are some of the customs of Chinese people today?

SUGGESTED READING
Reading Expeditions
Civilizations Past to Present: China